Made To Be Intimate

A Christian's reflections on premarital relationships

Made To Be Intimate

A Christian's reflections on premarital relationships

Tom Ogal

Copyright © 2013 Tom Ogal
ISBN: 978-9966-1693-0-3

All rights reserved

No part of this publication may be reproduced, distributed, or transmitted in any form or by any means, or stored in any database or retrieval system, without the prior written permission of the author and Sahel Publishing Association.
The author assumes full responsibility for the research, Bible quotations and all content of this book

Published by Sahel Publishing Association,
a subsidiary of Sahel Books Inc.
P.O. Box 18007—00100
Nairobi, Kenya
Tel: +011-254-715-596-106
www.sahelpublishing.net

A Sahel Book

Editor: Sam Okello
Interior designed by Hellen Wahonya Okello
Cover designed by Hellen Wahonya Okello
Printed in India, UK, U.S.A

To the memory of my late dad, Arthur, and to my mum, Nereah, for training me in the way I should go; and to my dear wife, Benter, who has taught me to appreciate that we were made to be intimate

Acknowledgement

There are many people I should thank for the help they gave me on this book. Without mentioning the specific help they gave me, I owe a lot of gratitude to my former teachers at the University of Eastern Africa, Baraton, Kenya, notably Professor Nehemiah N. Nyaundi, Dr. Elijah E. Njagi and Professor Denford B. Musvosvi. I am also indebted to my former student colleagues at the same university who were willing to share with me the nature of premarital relationships in their communities. These include Arizona Baongoli Mungengo, from the Democratic Republic of Congo, Mbaasa Batalingaye, from Uganda, Moses Mulongo, from Kenya, Kingsley Matiti, from Malawi, Passmore Mulambo, from Zambia, and Maima Zazay from Liberia. Being aware that I may not be able to mention the name of every individual who aided the writing of this book, allow me to just say a sincere "thank you" to those whose names I have mentioned and to those whose names, without any malice meant, I have been unable to mention.

TABLE OF CONTENTS

Dedication 7

Acknowledgement... 9

Introduction 13

One
By way of definitions... **17**
What is dating?.. **17**
Casual dating... **21**
Serious dating.. **23**
Dating defined... **25**
The rationale for dating.. **26**
God's will in dating... **31**
General trends in dating...................................... **37**

Two
The nature of boy-girl interactions in Africa............... **43**
The dating scenario in the past............................ **43**
The dating scenario today.................................... **45**
Journey through selected African communities........... **47**
The rural scene.. **54**
Urban scene.. **56**
Putting an African face to dating........................ **58**

Three
Dating and premarital sex.................................... **60**
Reasons for upsurge in premarital sex.................. **61**
Arguments for premarital sex............................. **64**

Arguments against premarital sex............................ **66**
The need for sexuality education........................... **69**
How can a young person stay pure?....................... **71**
Taming the fires of sexual passion........................ **72**

Four
Common problems in dating................................ **74**
Problems of intimacy.. **74**
Taking advantage.. **76**
The problem of getting dates................................ **78**
Date rape... **79**
Unplanned dates.. **85**

Five
Dating and mate selection..................................... **86**
The process of mate selection................................ **87**
The young man's shopping list.............................. **89**
The young lady's shopping list.............................. **91**
Breaking up... **93**

Six
Are you ready to tie the knot?.............................. **96**
How to differentiate true love from infatuation?........ **97**
Gauging compatibility... **100**

Seven
Wrapping up.. **102**
How do you know you've met the special person?..... **103**

Point to ponder.. 105

Introduction

Every society has its norms and values pertaining to every aspect of life. In this respect, intimate relationships and interactions between males and females, whether marital or premarital, are no exception. This is true of every society, the African society included. The traditional experience in many African communities as pertains to intimate, premarital male-female relationships was such that there was usually very limited and often closely guarded interaction between young people of opposite sex.

This norm has and does continue to change owing to the rapid social and cultural changes that have and are still taking place in Africa and elsewhere. These changes have brought with them a lot of liberty in all spheres of life. As a result, it is not uncommon anymore for young males and females to spend much time together; alone and away from the watchful eyes of parents.

The Western-style of dating has and continues to gain currency in Africa at a fast pace. African youth are coming out of their huts, as it were. Consequently, there is an unprecedented upsurge in sexual activity among the youth.

The kind of society that the youth find themselves in is one that is in a state of confusion. Society today, it would appear, attaches status to a young man showing evidence of being what can rightly be called a 'sexual athlete.' Young men are supposed to, in the eyes of their peers at least, have a string of girls running after them in order to qualify to be regarded as "real men." More than that, they are supposed to know everything about sex so that one should feel out of place to claim that he has never engaged in sexual intercourse with a lady. Similarly, it is almost considered abnormal for a teenage lady to still be a virgin.

It is this state of confusion that has lead many young people, especially in the rural areas of Africa, to equate dating with sex. It is often that I hear many young people say, "I have a date on such- and-such a day" when all they actually mean is that their girlfriends are visiting for nothing other than sex.

The idea of writing this book is borne out of a desire to share some insights on the nature of male-female relatedness with the youth in Africa in particular, and elsewhere in general. These insights, shared from an Afro-Christian perspective, it is hoped, will not only be helpful, but also useful in affording the reader an understanding of dating in particular, and human intimate relatedness in general, in such a way that it's true beauty and nobility can be fully appreciated by Christian youth.

The thrust of this book is to try to show that dating is not only healthy, but is important in the process of building sure foundations for marriage. Dating provides a kind of learning experience, which enables those involved in it to learn to appreciate not only themselves, but other individuals as well. This appreciation of the other individuals proves valuable later in marriage. That Christian youth, even in the villages of

Africa, can engage in socially and emotionally healthy premarital relationships, is a contention presented with considerable emphasis in this book. This book highlights the fact that some of the problems of marriage can be curtailed through dating, since dating should play an important role in mate selection. It has been observed that most marriages experience problems due to incompatibility, which may sometimes be a result of poor mate selection.

I do not purport to argue that healthy dating can perfectly eliminate all the problems that are experienced in the marriage institution, but I submit that it should be able to ensure that marriage is entered into on a sound premise thus minimizing the problems.

To be better able to achieve the purpose of writing this book, I have chosen to be deliberately liberal in my use of language. Some of the facts that compose this book are drawn from the impressions that I have formed from the readings of literature dealing with this topic. My experiences growing up as a young Christian in a rural African environment, coupled with the ideas I gathered from talks with some African young people from different countries on the continent with whom I have had opportunity to interact, also find expression in this book.

It is my hope that this effort will be able to impart invaluable knowledge, first and foremost, to my fellow Christian youth in Africa, and also to Christian youth elsewhere as well. It is also hoped that this book will be able to help Christian young people living in environments similar in one way or the other, and yet at the same time different in a myriad ways from mine, to stand pure in spite of the pressures of our anatomy and physiology; young men and women whose experiences and struggles through the turbulent and critical years of youth may be more or less similar to mine.

Finally, this book makes no claim to being a final word on the topic of dating and premarital relationships, leave alone being an adequate treatment of this wide subject. However, I believe that it has a worth that can be discerned by any keen and purposeful reader. The purpose of writing this book shall have been achieved if it should speak to the needs of its readers thereby, helping them to appreciate the beauty of healthy dating, guided by Christian principles.

Chapter One

Before dating is defined

Since this is a book dealing with premarital relationships, I devote a lot of attention to dating as a form of premarital relationship. It is thus that I want, at the very outset, attempt a definition of dating. Equally important is the need to present some general features that characterise the dating scene and which can be aptly thought of as the identifying marks of the dating game. This chapter therefore seeks to answer such questions as: what is dating? What are its features? Does God approve of dating?

By way of seeking to answer these questions, two stages of the dating process are discussed before moving on to present a working definition of dating, as it should be understood in this book. I have then proceeded to discuss the rationale for dating. An attempt is also made to discern God's will in dating. A brief discussion of the contemporary trends in dating concludes this chapter.

What is dating?

It is not easy to define dating because the term is used in a variety of ways, depending on an understanding of the people involved. To some people, dating means "sex" as has been hinted to in the introduction. To others, it means a relationship between a girl and a boy or between a man and a woman, not so much as pertains to their going out together, but as is seen in the way they interact, although going out is a common feature. To such people, dating is a process of interaction. It is a relationship.

Defining dating is further made difficult by the close link that has been woven between dating and courtship. While it must be admitted that there seems to be no clear-cut distinction between dating and courtship, let me say that dating is, first and foremost, about friendship rather than marriage. Courtship, on the other hand, is specific and comes much later after two people are well acquainted with each other and have made decisions based on the understanding that they have enough reasons to link their lives in a life-long union.

In spite of what I have just said in the paragraph above, I am well aware that there are those who will find problems with my argument that courtship follows dating. For the purposes of this book, however, I intend to keep this line of thought so as to help bring out the difference between the two. I take courtship to be the other side of dating. Courtship can, in many ways, be considered to be the serious side of dating.

Another reason that makes it difficult to define dating is the fact that there is no general agreement as to when dating should begin. The age at which dating begins often plays a leading role in determining the behaviour patterns of those involved and in essence gives another face to dating. Defining dating is, therefore, made complicated by the different patterns or faces that it assumes. Dating, in the real sense of the word, begins quite early in life. In this book, however, it should be understood that the age at which dating should begin is not determined so much by the chronological age of those involved, but by their emotional and mental maturity. At the same time, this book dwells on dating as is practised by people who are old enough to make important choices and crucial decisions for themselves.

There are many young people who wait until they feel that they are ready to get married before getting to have any meaningful and intimate interaction with members of the opposite sex. For such, dating only begins after they have fixed their eyes on marriage and, in most cases, when the mate has already been selected. Sometimes there are those who will wait until after they have entered into a commitment to marry before they begin to date.

The form of intimate relatedness that takes place between a young man and a young woman in the period after an agreement to be married has been entered into is generally referred to as courtship. The word courtship comes from the word "court" which has the synonyms adulate, allure, attract, cajole, cultivate, entice, pursue, romance, solicit and woo. The synonyms make it abundantly clear that the primary role of courtship is to achieve oneness between the courting young people. Such oneness can only be made complete in marriage so that courtship has marriage as its goal. This is opposed to dating where marriage may or may not be considered.

The major purpose of dating is socialization, though often, dating functions in many ways as a process of selecting a life partner for many people. With these in mind then, we can say that dating is not courtship, although dating often continues well into the engagement and courtship period.

It is important to be aware of what dating really is, and of the difference between it and courtship, because there are many who have related blindly, unsure of how to define their relationship; whether they are courting or just dating each other.

As the dating relationship passes from one stage to the next, from the casual phase to the serious phase, it is important that those involved know exactly where they stand, and what the future holds in store for them together if the heartaches often caused by mistaken and misunderstood signals and messages are to be avoided.

The most pronounced feature of the courtship period is the desire to get to know each other better, since at this stage those involved have focused their eyes on marriage. Dating, therefore, it should be understood, is not courtship and should begin well before an engagement is entered into. To equate dating with courtship is to miss the point. This is so because it is true that the real beauty and freedom that characterizes the dating period cannot be fully experienced when two people have already set their minds on what they want to do with their lives together. The freedoms that are inherent in dating must, however, go hand in hand with responsibility, and must be guided by the Christian sense. Again, before attempting a definition of dating, it would be helpful to, at this stage, discuss two phases of dating. These are casual and serious dating. The way I have handled these two forms of dating in no way purports to represent the meanings attached to them by all people. What is casual for one person may not be so casual to another. Likewise, what one person considers serious; another person may not regard so. It is thus, that many young people find it difficult to say with certainty which stage of dating they are in. However, there are general characteristics that mark these phases of dating, and these are the features that I seek to highlight, so that the reader may be helped to understand the meanings of these different features that surface as the relationship develops.

Casual dating

Casual dating may be better understood as an informal interaction between people of the opposite sexes. Often, but not exclusively, casual dating simply involves a coming together of a group of individuals for a common activity such as to play a ball-game, have a party, listen to music, watch a movie, go for a walk together, have lunch together, study together, among others. This may sound to many as typically Western. The truth is that many African young people are engaging in this kind of dating.

Casual dating involves no commitment and often a group of people are involved. This does not, however, mean that two individuals cannot go out together for any of the events already mentioned. It would be an error to say that casual dating strictly involves groups. The meaning is found in the root of the word "casual" not in the number of people involved. The bottom line in casual dating is that there is no commitment and no partner feels let down in the event of loss of interest in the relationship by either partner.

Casual dating provides opportunity for two people who might be interested in each other to get to know one another better. Let us take the example of a young man meeting a lady at a social gathering, or while travelling in a bus. They chance to have the opportunity to engage in talk, and in the course of their talk, they get to discover that they have a number of common interests. The guy ends up asking the girl for a "date" and the girl says yes. This marks the beginning of a casual relationship between the two.

As time goes by, their interest in each other grows and they begin to spend more and more time in the company of each other, provided that the economic, geographical and social factors are in their favour. Their friendship gets stronger and stronger by the day. The appropriate term to use here is probably "steady," so that it can be said, "so and so are getting steady." With the continued passage of time, they become more attached, especially emotionally. They may begin to think of marriage and make moves in this direction. Should this be the case, they graduate from the casual to the serious dating stages, before entering engagement.

It should be noted, however, that not all casual dates move into the serious dating stages. We will look at some of the reasons for this in the following pages.

Serious dating

The serious phase of dating differs from the casual phase in several distinct ways. First and foremost, the serious phase of dating does not begin overnight. It is the culmination of a long period of friendship and casual interaction, even of some amount of study, as has already been discussed above.

The term "serious" here means that the young man and the young lady now choose to date no one else except themselves, unlike during the casual dating stage when the guy or the girl can date others. It means that the two are now keen on, and are beginning to be aware of the destination of their relationship. This phase of dating is characterized by feelings of love and deep affection. Such feelings are not only recognized, but are reported. The partners are more interdependent and realize how much they need each other. They long to spend hours on end in each other's company.

The serious phase of dating, it has been observed, is also marked by an increase in conflict and negativity. This may sound rather strange and one may ask: "why?" The answer is simple. The conflicts are the result of differences in values and personality traits. Such differences and conflicts are perfectly all right if they are not blown out of proportion, for the truth is that a serious relationship that experiences no differences might be full of infatuation and devoid of reality. This phase of dating is one of serious study and the partners want to know each other better. They want to be sure that the premise upon which they want to build their future together is not faulty or deceptive. As a result, things that may have remained hidden before are thus brought to the surface. Character and values, some of which would be overlooked during the casual phase of dating, are put under close scrutiny, and generally, there is more concern by both partners as to what happens to the other, or what the other does.

This stage in the dating process is similar to courtship in a number of ways. One notable similarity is that during this phase of dating, as in courtship, the question of compatibility is given serious consideration.

Each partner asks, "Can I link my life and destiny with this man or this lady? Can we face the challenges of life together? Are we suited for each other? What has the future in store for us together?" This should emphasize the fact that the question of compatibility is one that is of prime importance in the contemplation of entering into a life-long union. It is one that must be put above such factors as physical attractiveness, for it will, to a great extent, determine whether the union will be a happy or unhappy one.

Another characteristic of the serious dating phase is that the partners get to learn and put in practice conflict resolution techniques. They learn how to work through their differences and get to a solution. The more they are able to sort out their differences, the more compatible they may be judged to be. Being able to resolve differences alone, however, is not the only sign of compatibility, though it weighs heavily in favour of compatibility.

Should a relationship survive the serious phase of dating such that partners become even closer and more committed to each other, then an engagement may be entered into, in essence ushering in courtship, which is the final phase in the long and sometimes turbulent journey through intimate premarital interactions. Successful dating and courtship is followed by the wedding, which marks the beginning of a new stage in the long course through intimate relationships.

Dating defined

After discussing the two phases of dating, it may now be appropriate to attempt a working definition of it. I am talking of a working definition because as has already been mentioned, dating means different things to different people and as such it may have as many definitions as people perceive and practice it. The definition given here should, however, be generally acceptable to many.

Dating may be defined as a process of interaction that affords people, usually of opposite sex, who are attracted to each other, opportunity to mix freely and get to become better acquainted either casually or in a more serious and intimate way. Generally, it is a form of premarital socialization that helps enhance the emotional, mental, spiritual and even physical health of those involved in it. Dating is a sociological phenomenon that helps in the building of friendships, and permeates the premarital interaction of any society's youth. Dating may further be defined as a process of socialization that enables those involved in it to acquire important social and relational skills.

While this definition may not be conclusive, it does serve, I hope, to enhance the understanding of dating as discussed in this book. The stress is on dating as a process that enables young people of different sex to mix freely and get to become better acquainted with each other, thereby learning to respect, not only themselves, but one another as well.

The rationale for dating
Dating fulfils a very important function in the lives of young people. These functions speak so strongly for dating that its rationale need not be argued.

Dating helps meet the recreational needs of young people. Youth is a transition period. As to such, young people find so much to contend against; so much that wears them down so that they need to find time for recreation. They need time to relax and enjoy themselves, and thereby be rejuvenated and fitted to face the challenges of living and service. Dating provides this opportunity for relaxation and enjoyment. It provides time off the daily chores when young people can retreat to places and moments of quietness and serenity and enjoy each other's company even as they enjoy the best of God's handiwork.

Dating, in itself, when practiced in a sober and healthy manner, can satisfactorily meet the entertainment needs of young people. There would be no need, therefore, for young people to seek pleasure from such unfulfilling places as discotheques, theatres and dance halls. Dating is a treatment for loneliness. In an impersonal society such as ours today, where the pressures of life weigh heavily on everyone's shoulders, it is not surprising that everybody seems to be concerned only with his or her own business. Our society today, many rightly lament, is a very lonesome, cruel and unkind place. Yet it is human nature to always seek friendship and companionship. Dating bridges the gap and provides the youth with opportunity to bask in the warmth of friendship and, thus, beat loneliness.

Man, it has been said, is a social animal. It is thus necessary that we learn social skills. Dating provides the opportunity for socialization, a process during which those involved get to master the art of conversation, learn the need for cooperation and a regard for others.

As youth socialize, they get to acquire a sense of belonging. They get to perceive themselves as appreciated members of the society in which they live. Dating in this sense then helps enhance self-esteem and self-actualisation.

It is true that as we relate to other people, telling them who we are and learning who they are, we get to discover ourselves. It has been observed that we can only understand the much about us that we are willing to reveal to others. This means that only as we relate to others can we grow mentally, emotionally and spiritually. Our personality development is influenced by our relationships with other people. This is one important function that dating performs in our growth. Dating provides an opportunity for those involved to try out sex roles. I am reminded here of what I participated in when I was a young boy of no more than twelve. My friends and I would go out, especially during the school holidays and over the weekends, to have fun. While out there, the girls would light fires and begin to "cook" different "delicacies" pretending to be mothers. Some of the boys would engage in building "houses" using sticks and mud, while others would go "hunting" pretending to be fathers. Still, some of the boys and girls who were a little older would pretend to be mothers and fathers by adopting the very young ones as their children. Using makeshift wheelbarrows, the "fathers" and "mothers" would employ a "driver" and have him "drive" them around the play area. They would sometimes have the driver push them away from the play arena pretending to be going on a journey. On their arrival back their "children" would meet them with songs to welcome "mummy" and "daddy" home.

It is only recently that I have come to appreciate that even this was a form of dating. During such occasions, we were afforded the opportunity to try out sex roles, which cannot be learnt in a vacuum, but in real life situations where people of both sexes are involved.

Sex roles, however, should not be understood in this context to include sexual intercourse. Sexual intercourse is the consummation of marriage and no one can afford to trivialize this special and noble divine gift. Sex roles here have to do with duties as relate to the expected functions of males and females in the home in particular, and society in general.

Another important function of dating is that it meets our need for love. Every one of us craves love. We all want someone to love us and someone we can love. In fact, without love the will to live diminishes, our vitality wanes and hopelessness creeps in.

On the other hand, we look vibrant and full of vigour when we love and are loved. Our physical, mental and social functioning is enhanced when our need for love is met. Love, or the lack of it, has torn the world of many people apart. It is not surprising to note that thousands of people commit suicide each year due to perceived or real lack of love. Civil law courts are convened to handle divorce and separation cases everyday; cases filed by people who think their love has failed and therefore want to have a fresh and new beginning. It is also true that mental hospitals are filled with people who, because of the want of affection they cannot find, have crossed the borders of sanity and into the world of insanity. Dating fulfils this human need for love, affection and acceptance.[1]

Dating is a learning experience. When young people involve in it, they acquire the valuable knowledge of how to relate in a healthy and moral manner with members of the opposite sex. In fact, it is a useful tool in the development of healthy heterosexual relationships. More than that, through dating, young people learn to appreciate other people for who they

---

[1] Nancy Van Pelt. *To Have and To Hold: A Guide to Successful Marriage* (Nashville, Tennessee: Southern Publishing Association, 1980), p. 27.

are. They learn to respect not only themselves but others as well. Such lessons prove important later on in marriage and in social life in general.

Today's parents are too shy to discuss sexuality with their children, a role which was effectively handled in many African societies by the grandparents during the storytelling sessions. The result is that young people are left to find out for themselves the facts about this important aspect of human life. Guided dating can sufficiently handle the question of sexuality education.

Successful dating provides a way out of some of the heartaches that result from the wrong choice of a marriage partner. Young people should find in dating a panacea for some of the ills that plague the marriage institution such as a breakdown in communication and misunderstandings, together with other causes of incompatibility. This is because dating provides opportunity to learn communication skills.

It is in dating that a young person gets to discover that there are people in whose presence it would not be possible to be happy and others in whose presence it would be possible to find lots of joy and laughter.

Even though there is a strong argument in favour of dating, it must be borne in mind, however, that even a good thing such as dating can be abused. We shall see in some detail how dating can be abused later in chapter three, where we consider the question of dating and premarital sex.

God's will in dating[1]

How can we know God's will in dating? Does God approve of dating? Is dating a sin?

A good starting point for a journey aimed at discerning the will of God in dating is to consider, first and foremost, God's view of human sexuality, for it is true that our interactions as male and female, whether marital or premarital, and especially as Christians, are often shaped by our attitude toward human sexuality. The answers we can give to the question "is dating a sin?" will be guided to a great extent by our perception of God and of His role in the building of human sexuality.

As we endeavour to find answers to these questions, let it be borne at the back of our minds, the fact that the God who said, "it is not good for man to be alone" is a God who never changes. It has never been His will that man, as male and female, should be alone. He is the God who ordained and is fully involved in human relationships. It is His desire that we would invite and allow Him to guide our human relationships—even the intimate interactions—so that He may help us to enjoy the privilege of intimate communion between man as man and woman.

---

[1] Some of the thoughts in this section are gleaned from the book, *The Theology and Ethics of Sex* by Sakae Kubo (Nashville, Tennessee: Review and Herald Publishing Association), 1980. See also, *The God of Relationships* by the same author and publisher, 1993.

Sexuality was part of God's design in creating man as male and female. Human sexuality, as far as God is concerned, is opportunity for humanity to grow and persist in love and faithfulness. God never intended that human sexuality should be viewed as a simple biological provision for the sole purpose of reproduction. Though the procreative function of human sexuality is important, it should be viewed more broadly as encompassing the dynamics of fellowship expressed in various forms of relationships and interactions between man as male and female; relationships that benefit the individual as well as the entire human society.

And yet it is very difficult for many people to perceive sexuality and holiness as going together. This is so because from time immemorial, sex has been painted as sin. There is the view that has depicted sex as being inherently sinful. This view holds that to be aroused sexually is part of the lust of the flesh and an indication that the body has not been brought under the complete rule of the Holy Spirit. I do not wish to get into the theology of this thought in this book.

Another concept of human sexuality is coded in the idea of the forbidden fruit. There are people who have intimated that the forbidden fruit Adam and Eve ate in the Garden of Eden was coitus. That Adam knew his wife Eve sexually is the whole idea of the forbidden fruit. But we know for certain that the fruit Adam and Eve ate could never have been "sex" for long before the fall, God had ordained sex, which indeed finds its essence in human sexuality. Let us remember that God said to Adam and Eve, "be fruitful, multiply and replenish the earth." This, God said before and not after the fall. Procreation could be possible only through heterosexual intercourse, and that is the way God intended it to be. The Bible also says that Adam and Eve were naked and they were not ashamed of it.

Shame, as far as sex is concerned, was never and has never been in God's vocabulary. God ordained sex, not as an end in itself, but as a consummation of the marriage covenant. He did not ordain sex for purposes of procreation only, as some people have argued, but He also ordained it for fulfilment and completing the oneness that is supposed to exist between man as male and female. The oneness that was, and is supposed to be the result of a union between a man and a woman, would not be complete without a union of bodies in an enjoyable, healthy and fulfilling sexual relationship.

The Bible, in Genesis 1:27, says that God created man in His own image and likeness. What this verse means is that humankind, as male and female, together make up the image of God. Man reflects the image of God because as male and female, though being independent, they have a natural tendency to want the company of each other. Man as male and female co-exist in a state of mutual belongingness and they are continually interlocked in one form or the other of interdependent relationships. That humanity bears the image of God is not only manifested in their being in relation with God, but also in their being in relation one with another. This is God's will for mankind. It should be noted that the state of mutual belongingness in which humanity is continually interlocked has no age limits. The young are as mutually interlocked as the old. Neither does this mutuality respect economic, social or cultural factors. The poor, those who occupy the lowest ladders in society, those whose cultures are regarded as inferior as well as those who regard their cultures as superior are all brought together in this realm of human relatedness.

The thrust of this book is not to prove whether God ordained sex or not. This is a book on dating and premarital relationships, and should be the last to concern itself with the sexual intimacies whose place is in marriage. But I must emphasize the need for us not to lose sight of the fact that our perception of divinity and human sexuality has an influence on our perception of human intimate relatedness. In discussing the will of God in dating, therefore, it is appropriate to consider seriously why divinity saw it necessary to put in place those components of our bodies, which make us sexual beings. Equally important is the need for us to discover how God would have us respond to our sexuality.

The argument here seeks to establish God's will in dating. This, as already has been said above, can best be achieved by first establishing God's will in human sexuality, or rather how the Christian should relate to the reality of his or her sexuality. It is not improper to say that God ordained healthy, responsible, moral and mature intimate relationships between male and female, whether marital or premarital. This is true because God could not ordain human sexuality and then prohibit the practice or practices that would help in the building of positive attitudes towards the proper functioning of our sexuality.

I have a burden, however, to be sure that I am not misunderstood to be saying that as human beings we should handle our sexuality with animal instinct. I must not be understood to be saying that because we are sexual beings, our sexual conduct should be as would indicate that we have no sense to separate the moral from the immoral for emotional and physical release, and for fulfilment, growth, completeness and procreation.

It would not be right to argue that God did not ordain dating. However, it would be right to argue that it is not God's will for His children to engage in certain activities that are detrimental to our physical, spiritual and emotional well-being. One such unsuitable and unhealthy activity is premarital sex.

Ellen G. White wrote that it is the privilege and duty of Christians to seek to refresh their spirits and invigorate their bodies by innocent recreation, with the purpose of using their physical and mental powers to the glory of God. She, however, warned that recreation as practised by Christians should not depict scenes of senseless pleasure, gratification, amusement and merriment taking the form of the nonsensical. Christians should conduct their recreation in such a manner as will benefit and edify those with whom they associate, thereby helping to better qualify all to more successfully attend to duties devolving upon us as Christians.[1]

While it is true that the Bible does not say much in any clear terms about dating, yet it is neither quiet about the form that male-female intimate interactions should take. Indeed, the Bible is quite frank on topics that deal with intimate marital, and to a certain degree, premarital male-female relationships.

The Old Testament books of Genesis, Exodus, Numbers, Leviticus, Deuteronomy and Ruth give vivid pictures of what form the interactions between man as male and female should take. But probably, the best picture is found in the book of *Song of Solomon*.

The book of *Song of Solomon* can rightly be referred to as a song of human love and companionship. It is an apt illustration and description of the beauty of intimate male-female relationships. In fact, one can say with conviction that it is possible to read lines that hint on dating in this book.

The picture that comes to mind when one reads many of the passages in *Song of Solomon* is one of a young male and a young female who are attracted to, and love each other dearly, out in the field on a date. The language of the book depicts scenery that is fairly romantic.

---

[1] Ellen G. White. *The Adventist Home* (Nashville, Tennessee: Review and Herald Publishing Association, 1952), p. 493.

It is doubtful that God would permit such lines as are found in several passages from the book of *Song of Solomon* to find expression in the Bible, which is His inspired word, if it was not His will that His people should, through their interactions and communion one with another, learn to commune with Him as God, and Father of us all. Our interactions should ennoble and better fit us for service to God and to our fellow humankind, even as we find joy in the companionship of one another. This, indeed, is the will of God in human intimate relationships, dating being no exception.

Dating should be steered toward serving God and humankind. It should afford those who engage in it a training opportunity to be more useful in society by being fully developed socially, emotionally, spiritually and physically. This is the will of God in dating.

General trends in dating
The trends and patterns of premarital male-female interactions in Africa are changing rapidly. This is due to rapid social, cultural and economic changes, which are taking place in the world today.

Trends in communication technology, the presence of automobiles, the existence of co-educational institutions, and the advent of the computer have given a new face to and influenced the trends in dating greatly. These trends, which appeared first in Europe and America, have spilled over into Africa. As a result, it is much easier for young people to meet and go out quite often today than a few decades ago. It is so easy for young people to get in touch that dates are sometimes simply arranged over the phone. Even the clothing industry has yielded to the trends in dating. Today, the way one is dressed can sufficiently tell the occasion. More than that, one can say that the appearance of the unisex has changed the behaviour and dress patterns in society, and this too has had a bearing on dating trends in the sense that dress, to an extent, determines conduct, and in essence will determine what takes place during the date.

Social and economic factors have also impacted forcefully on the dating trends. Young people tend to choose the people they date within their social and economic brackets. It has been observed that young people from families of lower sub-economic status begin forming intimate relationships with members of the opposite sex late, while those from families of higher sub-economic status begin dating much early in their adolescence.

To be better able to understand the trends in dating in Africa, it is important, therefore, to note the new conditions under which modern young males and females are brought up. The Western style of formal education has brought about longer dependency of the male and female on parents unlike in the past. There has been considerable erosion of what used to be uniquely male habitats. Women have invaded areas which used to be predominantly male domains. Men too are invading habitats which were traditionally considered predominantly female spheres. The modern arena of intimate relationships, including dating, courtship and marriage, depicts a number of peculiar trends. First, there is delay of marriage in pursuit of career and education. Second, there is a general lack of personal constraint in sexuality, particularly by boys; the majority of whom consider premarital sex perfectly all right. Lessened moral orientation in the home and family is evident.

Girls, more than boys, seem to be setting their priorities upside down. Instead of falling for things that last, they often opt for temporal pleasure and excitement, falling for external beauty of character. It is thus that girls are obtained from "anywhere" and brought home for a few moments of pleasure before being dumped to nurse their hurt. This is a very common phenomenon in our society today.

Sex in the bush, which was a common phenomenon in many African communities a couple of decades ago, is, however, dying out. Unfortunately, this seems to have been replaced by an unprecedented culture of licentious sexual promiscuity and immorality.

It is true, then, that the meaning of love has been trivialized so that it is not uncommon to hear a young man say to a lady "I love you" when all he desires from her is her body. One wonders why the young man should say "I love you" instead of saying "I want to use you," for that is exactly what many young men have often meant by the "I love you" phrase. The result of the sexual permissiveness prevalent in our society today is seen in the fact that we have more and more teenage fathers and mothers who are ill prepared for the duties of parenthood. Education has alienated some young people from the traditional values system and the old ways of life. The families' socialization role has changed greatly. Today the young are left on their own to find out the facts of life by trial and error. There is need for instruction on sexuality. The existence of single-parent families has contributed to this trend of things in society, since most single parents are barely able to exact the kind of moral influence on children as dual parent families would be able to.

As has already been mentioned elsewhere in this chapter, it is easier for young men and women to meet these days than in the past. They meet in buses, in church, at school, at the market centre, at dance, music and cinema halls. Some of them live in the same neighbourhood or estate. Whereas in the past it was forbidden to see girls and boys loitering together in the streets, today it is not a taboo, more so in the urban areas. In fact, it is the practice.

Economic considerations also have a bearing on the trends of dating in Africa. Some girls prefer to have a boyfriend with a steady and high income to milk his money. It is, therefore, unlikely that such a young man would associate with such a girl just for companionship. At the back of the young man's mind must lurk the idea that he must reap as much as he is putting into the relationship.

A disturbing trend in the boy-girl relationships these days, as is discussed later in chapter two, is that the girl is invited to the boy's home for hours of sexual pleasure. Many of them meet at the boyfriend's home because it is more convenient that way. Few parents are aware that their daughters are engaged in such steamy affairs because they are not meant to know. In contrast, in the past the clan monitored behaviour of its youth. This has, regrettably, changed. Indeed, erosion of the moral order and restraint once exerted by Christian principles has allowed the image of human sexuality in Africa to take a beating. Colonialism, labour migration, urbanization and modernization have dissolved the old controls and undermined the meaning that sexuality had in our tribal cultures. There is a general decline in parental control and a decrease in community scrutiny of the young people. Coupled with this is the seeming wavering role of religious doctrine in controlling the process of sexual awakening. Further still, contraceptives have reduced the risk of unwanted pregnancies with the result that there is an upsurge in premarital sex.

Then, there is the influence of the television, with its apparent promotion of the sexually provocative body even in commercial advertisements. Published magazines also have a stepped-up erotic content of nudity and the sexy look on their cover pages and also in the inside pages.

As a result of the foregoing, new fashions in adventure and sexual relationships have taken over. Many young people find themselves under increased pressure to be precocious in "falling in love with" persons of the opposite sex. African youth are coming out of the hut, as it were, so much so that we can no longer ignore the reality of Western style dating even in the villages of Africa. Holding of hands, hugging, and kissing in public is not to be abhorred anymore. Such behaviours have taken root in the cities and institutions of higher learning in Africa and are quickly becoming the norm even in the rural areas.

In today's society, the Christian youth is at crossroads. He or she is faced with a lot of questions relating to intimate interactions between males and females. What difference should people notice in the dating patterns of Christian youth as opposed to the dating patterns of non-Christian youth? Is there a need to come up with a style of dating that respects our African orientation and which is, at the same time, tied to Christian principles and is best suited to our environment? How can Christian youth, living in the countryside where blood-ties predominate so that the member of the other sex one meets everyday is either a cousin or a brother or a sister, enjoy the beauty of dating? A rigorous attempt is made to answer some of these questions in the chapters ahead.

Chapter Two

The nature of premarital interactions in Africa

This chapter presents a comparative picture of the different forms that premarital relationships take in different African communities. The information presented here should serve to give a general picture of dating in Africa through the 1970s to date. The African communities from which the information are drawn may not represent the nature of premarital interaction patterns in the better percentage of African communities, but nonetheless it is information that should, in many ways, present a true picture of the form premarital male-female relatedness has taken in many parts Africa.

The dating scenario in the past

The concept of dating, as we know it today, is new to Africa. In the past, there was no dating in the sense that we understand it today in many African communities. In fact, such practices as would give rise to close and intimate interaction between the youth of opposite sexes only occurred under the hawk-like observing eyes of adults. In some African societies, girls were married off when they were still very young, mostly on reaching puberty.

If what existed in traditional Africa had any semblance of what might be called dating, then it is safe to say that in traditional societies dating took place in the form of traditional dances and social gatherings.

In the olden days the sense of kinship, which is unfortunately dying out today, was a very strong element in the African family structure. It made members of the family identify closely with one another, so that the boy-girl interactions were guided by these familial attachments. This is probably the one reason why in many African communities there existed little interactions between boys and girls, except during traditional festivals and ceremonies; for the boys and girls often had blood-ties one way or the other.

A common characteristic of many African societies is that it was a taboo for a parent and child to discuss sex. Sex was regarded with awe and an almost religious piety, and was not to be mentioned until one was ready for marriage. It was then that the parents would go about searching for a suitable wife for their son. In most traditional African communities, it was not unusual for marriage arrangements to be made without the knowledge or consent of the young man involved, at least in the initial stages of the negotiations. Sometimes marriage arrangements were entered into even before the birth of the people whose marriage was being arranged.

The picture portrayed is that young men and women were not to act independently on such important matters of the heart. It was assumed that they should know nothing about intimate male-female relationships until the time they would enter into such relationships through marriage. Grandparents always did a good job teaching the young people about their sexuality and reproduction, but even this with a lot of caution. The way grandparents taught lessons on sexuality might have been lacking in many respects. This always left room for the desire to experiment. Stories of young men "invading" the huts where girls slept were common in many African communities.

The dating scenario today
The dating scene in Africa today, as in the past, presents few variations from one community to another. Many peculiar similarities may be discerned, but there are also some distinct differences. A number of factors are responsible for the prevailing nature of boy-girl relationships in Africa today: colonization, Africa's interaction with Western imperialism and missionary activities marked the beginning of change in behaviour patterns from traditional norms to something alien to many African communities. Such interactions contributed to the emergence of the behavioural environment that we have in Africa in this day and age.

The role played by co-educational institutions in the shaping of boy-girl interaction patterns in Africa cannot be touched lightly when discussing the factors that have helped build Africa into what it is today. Education has helped shape the African society, not only politically, but also culturally, socially and economically. But it is probably the coming of the Western-style education, more than anything else, which has shaped boy-girl relationships in Africa into what they are. It can be said that the coming of schools brought boys and girls together, thus enabling them to interact more often. Other factors that have had influence on boy-girl interactions, generating the picture we have today, are economic, geographical, religious or social. But growth in urbanization and technological development has also influenced the nature of such relationships greatly.

To complete the picture, we must add the AIDS pandemic. The AIDS pandemic has had its share of influence on the nature and patterns of boy-girl interactions in Africa and elsewhere. It has, to an observable extent, led to some decline in promiscuity.

Today, boy-girl interactions in Africa exhibit features which are similar in many ways to Western-style dating. These days contact between young men and young women often involve spending money. Dating involves what has come to be understood as a "treat" so that the young man and the young lady re supposed to give each other a treat. Young men have come out of their huts, and together with the young ladies, have invaded the dance and cinema halls, the theatre, the bar and restaurant, the hotel and even the lodge.

Schools, colleges and university campuses have proved to be fertile grounds for dating. One would be missing out on something important to be in college or university and be "chilling out" of the dating scene.

Another characteristic that features prominently in the dating scenario in Africa today is the prevalence of premarital sex. Teenage pregnancies are increasing at an alarming rate. Probably this, more than anything else, has helped create the impression that the youth cannot be trusted to be responsible in their interactions as male and female. It is for this reason that many parents are weary of allowing their daughters to enjoy the company of men. Young people must reverse this impression if the idea of dating is to wash with the old folk. They must prove that they can be responsible and moral in their interactions.

Journey through selected African communities

Among the Luo of Kenya, boy-girl interactions were very limited in scope, often characterized by no more than casual interactions. Boys and girls were not allowed to spend much time together sharing any intimacies. If the interactions that took place between the boys and the girls could be considered in any way as some form of dating, then it only took place in the form of their meeting at the traditional festivals and ceremonies. Otherwise, one can say with certainty that boys and girls lived in two different worlds; they lived in worlds of their own as it were.

But in spite of these restrictions, boys and girls had ways of meeting and "doing their thing" without the knowledge of their parents. Their meetings were always shrouded in secrecy.

A typical rural scenario in the 1970s and early 80s could run something like this: a boy meets a girl and they arrange that the boy "collects" the girl. The boy would collect the girl from her place, often at night, and bring her home for a few hours of sex. At dawn, he would see her back to her place.

The girl would wake up in the morning and the parents would be deceived that she spent the whole night at home, not knowing that the girl spent the night with a man. Here is the form the conversation would take:

Boy: I would like to talk to you.
Girl: Talk to me about what?
Boy: You have no reason to be rude to me.
Girl: I am not being rude to you. Just tell me what you have to say and let me go. Someone I respect might find us standing here.
Boy: Okay, could I see you tonight? We would not have to worry about people seeing us then.
Girl: No, you can't. My father is so harsh. I can't leave home at night.
Boy: No, he won't know. I'll come when your old folk are asleep. And I'll ensure that you are back before they wake up.
Girl: But I am still scared. What if my father wakes up in the middle of the night and finds that the gate is unlocked? He would obviously suspect that somebody has gone out of the homestead!
Boy: Come on! Don't worry about your father waking up. He won't wake up I'm sure.
Girl: Okay. What time will you come?
Boy: Between ten and eleven. I'll whistle as I pass by the homestead so that you would not mistake who is there.
Girl: I must go now. See you then.
Boy: See you.

That girls and boys were not to interact in public can be illustrated by the fact that a young man could run into the bush to avoid meeting his mother, father or any other significant person in his life such as an uncle, an older brother or an older cousin while in the company of a girl.

The above picture among the Luo is true in several African communities. The Bakonzo, who live in western Uganda, on the foot of Mount Ruwenzori, like the Luo, made sure that there was very little unsupervised interaction between boys and girls. Relationships were jealously guarded. Parents arranged marriage. Sometimes, and this happened often, they made the arrangements without consulting the young people involved at all, because the young people were assumed to be unknowledgeable about male-female intimacy.

The Bakonzo ostracised any girl who became pregnant out of wedlock. Such girls were banished into the wilderness. This was aimed at making sure that girls avoided and dreaded boys, especially those who made any sexual advances the same way they would dread a scorpion. As a result, the worlds of the boys and the girls were pushed farther and farther apart.

Again, what has been said of the Luo and the Bakonzo can be said of many other African communities. The Bangala, of the Democratic Republic of Congo, however, present some peculiar features. Although the Bangala, like many other traditional African communities, were weary to let young people of opposite sex engage in intimate interactions, they nevertheless had a practice that, in many ways, enhanced dating. Let me explain this.

Since the Bangala lived along River Zaire, they practised fishing. Young people could go fishing in groups of girls and boys. Sometimes they took advantage of the "fishing together" privilege to engage in premarital sex. This was illicit, though. Then it gets more interesting!

What was licit among the Bangala in so far as boy-girl interaction were concerned was called in the vernacular *kanga lopango,* which literally means "closing the gate." *Kanga lopango* was a token given to the parents of the girl by the family of a boy who had shown interest in marrying the girl. It was sometimes given in the form of fish and was never treated as bride wealth. The main reason of giving *kanga lopango* was to enable the boy and the girl interact more closely so that they could get to gauge their suitability for each other in a lifelong union. Such interactions sometimes went a little far to include, and unfortunately so, engaging in premarital sex. It was some kind of trial marriage.

The giving of *kanga lopango* was, therefore, aimed at ensuring that the girl did not see other men except her "husband-to-be." It put some kind of "booked" tag on the girl. The "booked" tag, however, never ensured that the two ended up getting married to each other. It was not always that the young man who had given *kanga lopango* ended up marrying the girl for whom he had given this token. Such engagements were often broken when a situation necessitated it.

The Bakongo, also of the Democratic Republic of Congo, displayed some very interesting features in so far as boy-girl interactions were concerned. It was permissible among the Bakongo for one to marry from or to be married within his or her extended family. What this meant was that cousins could marry each other. Owing to this, boy-girl interactions among the Bakongo were not restricted as among other African communities. Such interactions began early, sometimes when the boys and the girls were barely in their teens. The Bakongo could, in many ways, therefore, be regarded as having been a very permissive society. Premarital sex was not uncommon. This should not, however, be taken to mean it was encouraged.

The nature of boy-girl interaction among the Lomwe, Chewa, Tumbuka, Yao and Sena of Malawi, the Tonga, Lenje and Ila of Zambia, the Ashanti of Ghana and the Shona of Zimbabwe does not differ much from the boy-girl interaction patterns displayed by the African communities already discussed above.

The Lomwe, however, cast a feature that deserves mention. Boy-girl interactions received parental nod. The condition, however, was that the young people could not stay out until very late. In fact, they were only allowed to go out between two o'clock in the afternoon and four, not more than two hours out. Boys and girls would be seen walking along the road chatting, chewing sugarcane, or just standing rather purposelessly by the roadside. The fact that boy-girl interactions among the Lomwe received parental nod does not imply any permissiveness. Like many other traditional African communities, these interactions were guarded very jealously.

Mention should also be made of a peculiar feature that characterized boy-girl interactions among the Shona, until a couple of decades ago. After a young man identified a girl he would want to "check out," he could use his sister to help him have access to the girl. He would have his sister befriend the girl so that through the sister, he could find out details about the girl. On occasions, the sister would invite the girl home so that the brother would have an opportunity to interact with her more closely. At the end of the visit, sister and brother would together see off their visitor. Though such interactions were supposed to preclude premarital sex, sometimes the young people could abuse the privilege the intimacy they enjoyed accorded them. The bottom-line, however, was to get to find out whether the girl was of marriageable character or not. This process of "checking out" did not just last a day or two; it lasted a couple of months or more. Parents would always have their suspicions, but since the interactions were in many respects carried out in a healthy and moral manner, they had no objections. Their counsel would, however, be sought, especially when it came to the finer details of arranging a marriage.

One other thing that should be mentioned about the nature of premarital male-female interactions among the Shona people, as among many other African communities, was the apparent double-standard that gave boys leeway to interact with "other people's sisters" but kept boys from making moves on their own sisters. In fact, stories of brothers warning or sometimes using brutal force to ensure that other men kept away from their sisters are not uncommon among the Shona, as well as among other African communities.

Though the nature of boy-girl interactions among the Ashanti of Ghana did not differ much from the patterns displayed among other African communities, one or two features that characterized such interactions among the Ashanti are worthy of consideration. One thing was that young men and young ladies entered intimate relationships only after they had set their eyes on marriage. The young men would wait for the ladies by the road on their way to or from the village well or the river. They would engage in some chatting, but there was always the fear of being found chatting by some significant other in the lady's life such as mother, father, uncle or aunt. As a result of this fear, the chitchat never lasted more than a couple of minutes.

However, after the two were certain that they had some fire going, they would be a little bolder in their interactions. The young man would occasionally go as far as the outskirts of the lady's homestead and send a word that he would like to see her. In fact, he would sometimes use the young lady's own brother as the emissary. After this had continued for sometime, the girl's parents would begin to have their suspicions. And so, one day the boy would send word to the girl to meet him, but the girl's parents would insist that the boy gets into the home. The boy would oblige. The relationship would, from this point forward, take a different turn. The boy and the girl would now be free to interact more closely and in public without any fingers being raised against their interaction. The girl would now be bold enough to invite the boy to take her to the farm; an invitation the boy would accept if he was keen on marrying the girl.

The rural scene
The youth in the African village is still trapped in a dilemma. This is because the people of the opposite sex he or she meets everyday is a sister, a brother or a cousin. It should be remembered that the concept of the extended family is still very strong in rural Africa. The dilemma then is: where shall the youth in the village find a date? Shall he or she date his or her sister, brother or cousin?

Again, the rural scene is lacking in the variety of activities that bring young people together. Those activities that young people would want to engage in during a date are lacking in the rural areas. There is no theatre, dance hall, cinema hall or park. Young people in the village meet at school, in church, at the village shopping centre, at the river or the lake when they go to draw water or to fish, in the forest when the boys take the animals to pasture and the girls go to collect firewood, during sporting activities and at the village social gathering, whether for a funeral or a traditional wedding. A notice that reads "disco dance and video show" posted on a shop window or a tree by the roadside evokes enthusiastic response from the village youth. Disco dance occasions present opportunity for the young men to meet the young ladies and take them home for an hour or two of sexual intimacy. It should be noted that parents are not supposed to be aware of their sons or daughters attending the disco dances. As such, these young people "escape" from home after the old folk are asleep and return before they are awake.

Boy-girl interactions in the rural areas are still very limited. Intimate relationships between the two often take the form of the sexual. They have not learned to stop treating each other as sex objects. Sex in the bush, though dying out, still has disciples. Today, the girl is brought home to the boy's hut unlike in the past when it was done in the bush.

As a result of the high prevalence of sexual activity among young people in the countryside, the prevalence of teenage pregnancies among village girls is equally high. This is true for many African communities. Consequently, abortion is also on the rise, the most common practice being the taking of an overdose of an unprescribed drug. This has cost the lives of many young girls.

Young people in the village are yet to fully appreciate and appropriate for themselves the beauty and nobility of moral and healthy dating devoid of preoccupation with sex. They have not learnt to enjoy the beautiful garb of nature, which in the rural areas has not been interfered with much and therefore retains much of its splendour.

Given the important functions dating fulfils in the lives of young people, the village youth in general and the Christian youth in particular can and should engage in healthy dating relationships, guided by moral and Christian principles. If this were to be the case, the traditional norm in many African communities that prohibited close association between boys and girls with familial ties would have become incongruent with reality. In other words, interactions between sisters and brothers, or between cousins, would thus be regarded as normal and moral, for the immoral shall have given way to the moral, and no sexual immorality would be seen in these interactions.

The urban scene
Dating patterns in the urban centres of Africa differ from the village patterns in many distinct ways. Dating in urban areas often involves activities such as going out to watch a movie or a play at the theatre.

Whereas in the rural areas, boy-girl interactions seemed to be centred around sex, this is not the case in the urban areas. It is true that even in the cities and towns young people engage in premarital sex, but it is not as an obsession as it seems to be in the rural areas.

The factors that have helped shape the dating patterns of young people in towns and cities are different from those that have influenced the dating patterns in the rural areas. The movie, the theatre and the dance hall are to a large extent the preserve of the urban areas. The general lifestyle in the cities and towns also has a bearing on the nature of boy-girl interactions in these urban areas. The picture that results from this is one that depicts boys and girls as beginning to date early, unlike their rural counterparts.

Urban-based youths do not find it difficult getting dates. Sometimes it is the girl who lives next door, or in the neighbourhood. Boys and girls meet at school, at church, at the supermarket, in the estate bus, on the streets, at the coffeehouse, at the dance hall, at the theatre, at the cinema hall or at a social gathering.

Since urban-based parents are in most cases more informed than their rural counterparts, some give their children permission to date. Boy-girl interactions in the urban centres are therefore not as shrouded in secrecy as they are in the rural areas.

Another picture of dating that comes from the cities and towns is the one that reveals a significant amount of necking and "pecking." A typical scene would cast a boy waiting for a girl at a given point. The girl arrives, allows the boy to wrap his arms around her and off they go to either the cinema hall or to the theatre. Holding of hands in public is also common.

Dating in the urban areas is, in some case, very formal. Sometimes dates are arranged over the phone. After agreeing on what time the boy is to meet the girl, the young man would use his daddy's car or his own, if he has one, to pick up the girl. Since most young people, especially the working class and those in school, are usually occupied during the week, the weekend is found to be the ideal time to go out.

The entertainment industry has caught up to this. It is thus that a lot of entertainment activities are lined up for the weekend. The theatre scene, the music scene, the cinema hall, the art scene and the recreational "hang out" are very busy over the weekend.

Most city or town-based youth celebrate occasions like Valentine's Day with pomp. The rural-based counterpart may not even know what St Valentines day is all about after all. As a result the urban culture, flowers splash the dating scene in urban centres. The romantic dinner out is not uncommon either.

From the foregoing, it is true to say that the dating patterns in the African city or town are in many ways very similar to the dating patterns in cities and towns in Europe and America.

Putting an African-Christian face to dating in Africa
Can there ever be such a thing as an African-Christian face to dating? This question finds its essence in the argument that dating, as it is practised today in Africa, is foreign to the continent. While this may be true to some extent, the reality is that boys and girls can no longer be banished to a world of their own. African young men can no longer be confined to their huts. What needs to be done is to put an African-Christian face to dating as practised in Africa.

It should be noted that the idea of socialization is not new to Africa. Indeed, the spirit of African socialism, which is deeply rooted in the heart of and psyche of the African, espouses the companionship and relatedness of man as male and female.

This is where it must all begin. The spirit of African socialism cherishes and upholds respect as is seen in the piety with which kinship ties are held. The spirit of African socialism teaches respect for the individual as an equal partner in the affairs of the community.

If this kind of respect were to be transferred to the dating scene, dating as a process of socialization would become a more readily acceptable, wholesome, fulfilling and growth-enhancing activity. Incest and premarital sex, which are incongruent with the African concept of morality, would cease to feature on the dating scene. There is thus an urgent need to emphasize traditional moral norms in the boy-girl interactions in Africa today and in the future.

Chapter Three

Dating and premarital sex

Is premarital sex wrong? Does God condemn it? What if we love each other and are intending to get married? What are the ill consequences of engaging in premarital sex? How about the idea of "practice makes perfect?" What if we get married and discover that we cannot fulfil each other sexually?

These and other related questions are grappled with in this chapter. I approach these questions with caution, first and foremost because I am fully aware that they may not be fully answered. I am also cognizant of the fact that since they are often uppermost in the minds of Christian young people in all places, they demand to be approached open-mindedly. Again I am also aware of the fact that there are differing and varied views on the issue of premarital sex.

Finding answers to these questions is made more difficult by the fact that we live in what can be described as the sex explosion age. Sex, even in its premarital form, is regarded as very normal and is engaged in without any consideration as to whether it is wrong or right. As a result it is rampant everywhere. Young people are bombarded with sexual overtones from both the print and electronic media.

The clothing industry has not been left behind either as it has evolved in what has been described as sexy fashions. It is unfortunate that even some films intended to teach Christian morals have taints of nudity and overt sexual lines.

Our society today has been described as permissive, licentious, reckless and vicious. Perhaps, this permissiveness has been seen in the area of premarital sex more than in any other area. Many young people will quickly dismiss their engaging in premarital sex with the excuse that everybody is doing it. It is unfortunate that even Christian youths seem to have embraced this attitude of permissiveness and recklessness wholeheartedly. Casual coitus seems to be the order of the day and those who are not doing it are made to feel like they are missing out on something important. The watchword is experimentation. Everybody wants to get a taste of how it feels.

It is this kind of permissive and reckless orientation that has, and continues to degrade the nobility of wholesome intimate relationships between young males and females. Intimate male-female interactions between the youth are today characterized by sexual intimacy. Many youths are deceived into think that engaging in coitus is the only way to cement their relationships. The unfortunate fact, however, is that sex, instead of cementing the relationship, in almost all cases, wrecks it.

Reasons for upsurge in premarital sex
One reason why there is an upsurge in premarital sexual activity is the desire to experiment. This desire is to some extent influenced by the way sex has been treated. Sex has

been regarded as a mystery. It is not something to be discussed or mentioned carelessly. The kind of attitude we have had towards sex is one that confines it to the realms of carnal lust. This has aroused a lot of curiosity and it is out of it that young people are driven to "check out" what the so-called sexual intimacy is all about.

Other reasons for the upsurge in premarital sex have to do with the kind of societies we have built. As already said above, we live in a very permissive and licentious society, one that seems to have lost its sense of morality. Sex talk seems to be the only conversation that elicits some excitement, especially amongst young people. The mass media has also played a role in helping create the sex explosion. It is everywhere: in the television, magazines, radio, and the fashion industry, among others. Nudity is cherished. Image building to enhance sex appeal is an obsession. Even commercial advertisements must have a sexual overtone to have an amount of appeal.

There is a lessened moral orientation of home and family. Our society today exhibits a general lack of personal constraint in sexuality. Our society is experiencing the development of a culture that thrives on sexual liberty and licentiousness.

Drug abuse, coupled with the apparent intense dissatisfaction with restraints required for a well ordered society, is also responsible for the upsurge in premarital sex, since it leads to recklessness and loss of self-control. Stories of young people getting drunk and doing things that they would not do if they were sober are many. A good example is illustrated below.

Mark was bored one evening and went out to the neighbourhood bar for a drink. There, he met Sue and they quickly struck a rapport. The drink soon began to get the better of them. "Let's go upstairs to my room," Sue suggested. Mark looked at the longing in her eyes and the temptation was irresistible. He quickly got up and took her arm. They were soon in her room and one can guess what happened next. However, after the sexual fires had pacified and Mark began to soberly consider what he had just done, he felt guilty and cheap. He was devastated by feelings of low self-esteem. He was mentally torn at the thought of yielding to the lures of a bar girl, something he would never have done were he sober. It is thus true that premarital sex is more prevalent among the youths who drink alcohol and abuse drugs than among those who don't.

Young people are not only rebelling against traditional norms and 'old' values, especially those pertaining to boy-girl interactions, but are questioning and rejecting them as well. Blood ties have been abused and incest is becoming some kind of "no big deal" affair.

Then we have peer pressure, which plays a significant role in the decisions made by young people. No one wants to miss out on anything. Everybody wants to be part of the crowd. Young people always crave to be recognized as "belonging" and not out of touch with the trends. And since being in touch often means doing what everyone else is doing, many young people indulge in premarital sex to prove that they are trendy.

Ignorance has also contributed to the high prevalence of premarital sex. Young people have been given a raw deal in so far as sex education is concerned. They are either given inappropriate education on human sexuality or are left to find out for themselves about this important aspect of their lives. Most of what they know about human sexuality is either learned from the magazine, the movie or from peers. It is little wonder, then, that young people enter sexual relationships without adequate and accurate knowledge of the emotional, psychological and physical effects of such intimate involvements. This is especially true of the rural areas as opposed to the urban areas, where young people are a little more informed given the environment in which they grow up.

Arguments for premarital sex

There are people, including some Christian, who argue that premarital sex is all right under certain circumstances. On the other hand, there are others who are completely opposed to premarital sex under any circumstance or reason. However, it is important to discuss the arguments that have been posited in support of premarital sex before discussing the arguments against it. It has been argued that coitus in general and premarital coitus in particular, has the nobility to cement a relationship that might otherwise be going through the doldrums; that sex has the capacity to intensify emotional attachment between the two people involved. This argument would seem to imply that intercourse has an adhesive ability to save a relationship that has turned sour. While this may be true in some cases, it is true that premarital sexual intercourse has destroyed many relationships.

Another argument that has been advanced in support of premarital sex is that it improves or enhances sexual performance. Some studies have reported that young people with premarital sexual experience seem to have a more fulfilling sexual experience later on in marriage. This is supported by the idea that practice makes perfect.

Love, it has been said, is as strong as death. Arguing from this point of view, it has been said that it is all right for two young people who love each other so much to engage in coitus even if they are not married.

Human beings are by nature pleasure-loving. Thus, in our search for pleasure, coitus has come to be regarded as a very pleasurable activity. Sex for the sake of pleasure has become the order of the day. Indeed, it has become a sport. Psychologists tell us that pleasure yields both emotional and psychological release, which when considering the pleasure-yielding potential of coitus would then be argued that sex, including premarital, performs an important function in affording emotional and psychological release.

Another argument that has been advanced in favour of premarital sex is that it enhances emotional and psychological development. The contention is that those who engage in premarital sex are apt to experience faster and less traumatic emotional and physical adjustment.

Arguments against premarital sex

Before presenting the arguments that have been advanced in opposition to premarital sex, I must hasten to say that any argument against premarital sex must take into consideration the nature of sexual fires deep within us. While discouraging promiscuity, we must also seek to offer suggestions on ways of handling these fires.

The most common arguments presented against premarital sex are: unwanted pregnancies and the possibility of contracting sexually transmitted diseases. To cling to these as the best deterrents to premarital sex, however, is to present only the consequences which are obvious. The real reasons for discouraging premarital sex have been avoided. We must look at those in a more open manner today.

As Christians, the best argument we can present against premarital sex is that it is morally wrong. To say that teenagers engage in it for wrong reasons is not far-fetched. It is true that the foremost reason why young people engage in premarital sex is to satisfy their sexual lust.

Sex is one of the objects in their wider search for pleasure. It would be foolish to reason that there is no pleasure in coitus, whether it is practised in the security of marriage or before marriage. But the pleasure derived from sex before marriage is short-lived. It only lasts the duration of the intercourse and its results could be disastrous.

Premarital sex could result in early, unplanned marriages, especially when a pregnancy occurs. The occurrence of a pregnancy would also necessitate the making of several crucial decisions. Such decisions would include whether to go ahead and have the baby or to terminate the pregnancy, whether to get married before the child is born or wait until after birth, among others.

In many African communities, conceiving out of wedlock was and still is a stigma. It exacts a guilty conscience and can have severe psychological and emotional effects.

There is the guilt of breaking societal norms and moral standards. The lady loses the respect of the society. She is looked down upon and regarded as a disgrace to the society. More than that, it has also been observed that the man often loses respect for the lady. That the lady should lose the man's respect is indeed a double standard, since it implies that the man overlooks his role in causing the pregnancy.

Extensive studies have indicated that those who experience promiscuous relationships before marriage are apt to enter extra-marital affairs later on in married life. This is true when it is considered in light of the English saying that habit is second nature. Promiscuity therefore becomes second nature to those who have learnt to thrive on it in their premarital interactions.

The heartaches that result when premarital affairs turn sour usually leave lasting impressions on the mind. The scars take long to heal.

It is not unusual to hear young people expressing their misgivings about sex in general and relationships with the opposite sex in particular. These are expressions of hurts and pains borne. These hurts and pains are often the result of engaging in premarital sex. They lead to a sense of insecurity, such that the one who has been hurt loses interest in relationships with the opposite sex and his or her sex drive is dampened. This, studies have shown, could lead to inhibited sexual performance and even frigidity.

Those who contemplate engaging in premarital sex should consider the personal, social, religious and psychological implications of their sexual conduct. Again, those considering engaging in premarital sex should further ask themselves the following questions: is my sexual behaviour acceptable to my personal principles? If I engage in premarital sexual intercourse, will I still like my partner and myself? Is my behaviour contributing to the upholding of social principles or is it contributing to the breakdown of moral principles? Am I willing to uphold social norms? Is my sexual behaviour in agreement with these norms? What is the teaching of my religion concerning proper sexual conduct? Am I willing to follow those teachings? Can I live with the feelings of guilt that may result from my sexual behaviour? What will I do in the event that a pregnancy results from my sexual conduct?

Need for sexuality education

Is there need for sexuality education? The answer to this question is yes. Since sexual adjustment is part of the process of adjustment of the whole person, sexuality education becomes necessary in order to help build an all-round person.

Young people are receiving a lot of distorted, though not necessarily false, information from the mass media about human sexuality. Proper sexuality education can help put these distorted pieces of information into proper perspective. This makes it abundantly true to say that the one very sensitive area where young people need proper guidance today is the wider concept of human sexuality and the narrower area of boy-girl relationships; and thus the proper place of sex.

Sexuality education is further necessitated by the conditions prevalent in our world today. One does not need to emphasize the fact that there is a high premarital school dropout rate, misuse of contraceptives and abortions.

The availability of conception-control devices seems to be encouraging premarital sex. The presence of the condom seems to have reduced the AIDS scare and the risk of unwanted pregnancies.

Young people in Africa and elsewhere are "sowing their wild seeds" as if they are engaged in some form of competition or are on a sowing spree.

Sexuality education is, therefore, an urgent need for Christian youth in particular and for all young people in Africa in general. Christian youth need to be made aware of the fact that sexual morality springs from a sense of caring and respect for others, and that it is such a sense of caring that should guide their intimate relationships.

Because sexual education must begin at home, parents are called upon now, more than ever, to take up the challenge and be the first educators. Parents should be well aware that the way they answer questions, how they act and how total sexuality is handled in the home forms an integral component of sexual education. Because of that, open communication about sexuality should be facilitated between parents and young people.

Sexual education should aim at promoting chastity and the development of mature and integrated persons. It should encourage the provision of accurate and balanced information about human sexuality. Such information would help reduce the anxieties and fears of young people relating to personal sexual development and feelings.

It has also been observed that sexual education can function to enhance the making of informed and responsible decisions on the part of young people, pertaining to sexual behaviour. Young people should be encouraged to explore and question their sexual attitudes and behaviour against the backdrop of personal, moral, social and religious principles. Sexuality education should be conducted in a context of faith, highlighting the sacredness and sanctity of sex. This way, an environment shall have been created that enhances the development of satisfying and healthy interpersonal relationships.

Through sexuality education, young people should be helped to come to terms with the fact that moral and religious values, and a sense of commitment must be present in all sexual encounters.

How can a young person stay pure?

The greatest questions, which many Christian young people contend with in contemporary society as relates to human sexuality, are those that are related to purity and chastity. In today's viscous and depraved world, these questions become more urgent. This is so because the twin virtues of purity and chastity seem to be finding their way out of our society at an alarming rate, and the cry and prayer of parents is that their children rediscover these cardinal life-guiding principles. But where does the search for purity and chastity begin?

It must begin with a desire and a resolution to stay pure and practice chastity. The saying, which states that where there is a will there is a way, is true. If it were the desire of a young person to stay pure, such a desire, backed up with resolute willpower, is achievable. This is not to say that achieving the desire to stay pure would be easy. No. To think so is to be conceited. Given the nature and potency of human passion, it would take quite a struggle to stay pure, especially in our world today, where there are more attractions to please the carnal nature than distractions to keep us away from worldly pleasure.

Yet there is provision for the Christian youth who has resolved to stay pure. When a young person appropriates for himself or herself the provisions of a life guided by the Holy Spirit; a life tuned to the instructions found in the Word of God made available in the scriptures, it becomes possible to walk in the paths of purity and chastity. This is the only way a young man can stay pure; by allowing himself or herself to be led by the Holy Spirit, and by following the instructions of the Word of God. The Psalmist wrote in the ninth verse of the one hundred and nineteenth Psalms thus: "How can a young man cleanse his way." The Psalmist's discovery remains the only way a young man/woman can stay pure.

Taming the fires of sexual passion

In discussing the ways through which young people can handle the fires of sexual desire, one needs to be very open-minded. This is so because these fires are not only real, but are very powerful. In fact, they are so powerful that they sometimes leave us confused and feeling helpless. And then, at the same time, they generate a lot of pleasure. The question, which must be answered urgently, therefore, is: how can we respond to these fires in such a way that we would be able to appreciate them as part and parcel of our being? How can we handle them in such a way that we would not find ourselves under their control? To be able to handle the fires of sexual passions that burn deep within us, we must develop a positive attitude as regards our sexuality. There are people who choose to ignore the reality of these fires, confining them to the realm of evil. For such people, to have sexual desire is an indication that one is being controlled by carnal, lustful nature. Whereas it is true that sometimes we allow our carnal nature to determine our sexual behaviour, it is also true that to have sexual desire is not necessarily inherently evil. On the contrary, sexual desire is part of our normal biological nature.

Let it be noted that God created our whole being; sexuality included. It is Him who built those fires in us and for a good reason. God put the sexual fires in us as an integral component of our sexuality and they are to remind us that we are functioning normally. These fires should not be trivialized because they play an important role in the fulfilment of our functioning when it comes to sexual intimacy in marriage.

Appreciating the fact that God built the fires of sexual desire in us will help us accept them as real and good. Thus, we will be able to respond to these fires not as some evil force within us wanting to force its way out, but as a healthy component of our being, which must not be suppressed, but rather be related to responsibly and morally. Our human nature is such that we are powerless to tame our sexual desire. We need to place ourselves in God's hands and pray that His will should be done in our lives. It is only in this way that we can be able to respond to these fires in a manner that is devoid of animal instinct.

Chapter Four

Common problems in dating

The problems that are experienced in the dating game are many and varied. Such problems include those that relate to intimacy, problems which result from one partner taking advantage of the other, problems related to the difficulty in getting dates, problems that occur due to lack of planning of the activities to engage in on a date and the problem of date rape among others.

Problems of intimacy

Problems of intimacy are a common feature in the dating game. These often manifest in the form of misplaced affections and mistaken "leading signs." One partner may be led to think that the other is involved emotionally and psychologically and is committed to the relationship when the opposite is true. Misplaced affections can result into a lot of heartaches and pain and can cause wounds that would take time to heal. When the time comes to say goodbye, one is left with unreciprocated affections to deal with. Feelings of rejection play nasty games with the mind and one is given to believe that he or she is unlovable, ugly, inadequate and unworthy. One tends to think that something is terribly wrong with him or her. Maybe I didn't press the right button at the right time! Maybe I just didn't read the signals correctly! I am such a wretch! I must have made a mistake involving myself in this thing emotionally! I will never be able to move again! I have been such a fool!

Common problems in dating—75

In any intimate relationship, especially male-female relationships, it is always important to recognize and report feelings just as they are. Both partners should be sure that they understand each other well and know exactly where they stand. This can only be achieved through honest and open communication of feelings and affections. Mistrust and the tendency to play games with oneself and with one another are incongruent with the desire to build healthy intimate relationships. Joys and sorrows, expectations and fears should be reported for what they are. Affections should be reciprocated if the relationship is to workout, but if one partner is not interested, then it is wise to let the other know early enough so that he or she is not caused a lot of hurt by feeling that he or she is being led on and then later on being shocked out of his or her fantasies. The following story illustrates how bitter the pains caused by misplaced affections can be.

Dave and Mary had been going out for about one year. All along, Dave had assumed that Mary was as involved as he was; he thought that Mary had as much affection for him as he had for her. He interpreted the acts of kindness Mary did to him as meaning she was committed to ensuring that the relationship worked out for them. But that was not true. Mary was only interested in a friendship without any strings attached, no romantic involvement. When Dave was finally brought to face the reality; when he was awakened from the dreamland into which he had slipped, he was broken. It is then that he realized how deeply he had involved both his head and heart in the relationship. He realized that he had placed his affections where they were not appreciated. He had to retrieve them and place them elsewhere.

Dating has the potential to blind those involved in it, especially when it comes to intimacy. If the problems related to intimacy in the dating game are curtailed, then levels of intimacy should be clearly defined. The partners need to be sure how far they can go, and what every act that is meant to express feelings means. Is it just a peck without any feelings attached or is he making a point? Is it just an ordinary embrace or is there more to it? Is it just an act of kindness or is it meant to whisper something to me? The look in her sultry eyes, the smile on his face, the rose that is sent on a special occasion, the note that is sent to whisper "you are on my mind," all these need to be clearly understood for what they mean if neither partner is to lament later, "I was such a fool!"

Taking advantage
This is another common problem in dating. By taking advantage, it means one partner abuses the rights of the other partner simply because the other person is helpless. Since boy-girl interactions often involve spending money, the one who spends the money may be led to think that he or she can do whatever he or she wishes to the other partner simply because "I footed the expenses." It is neither moral nor Christ-like to take advantage of a fellow human being, especially someone you are dating. It has been observed that those who allow others to take advantage of them often have low self-esteem. They feel inadequate and think they cannot

live without the other person. It is thus that they allow their partners to trample on their rights as long as they keep the relationship going. All they are interested in is the survival of the relationship. The truth, however, is that such a cold relationship cannot survive very long. Sooner or later the one taking advantage begins to despise the other and relate to him or her with contempt. He/she begins to treat the other like a dog.

The taking of advantage may at times take the form of sex. Oftentimes, it is the lady who is taken advantage of sexually. It is also true that the tradition has been for men to take care of the expenses incurred during the dating activity. These two facts combine to give rise to the statement that the lady is often under pressure to reciprocate or pay back in kind for the expenses incurred by the man.

It is sometimes necessary that if the problem of taking advantage is to be avoided, the partners should work out a way of handling the expenses in such a way that nobody will feel obliged to pay the other back. This is not to say, however, that all men will always attach any strings to their taking care of the expenses. There are many who will simply do the "paying" because it is the gentlemanlike thing to do.

The best way out of the problem of taking advantage is for those who feel they are taken advantage of to work on their self-esteem. There is a lot of literature dealing with the building of self-esteem. In this way, they will be able to say no to acts that infringe on their rights.

The problem of getting dates

This is more often in the African rural areas than in the towns and cities, since, as mentioned in chapter two, in the rural areas blood ties play a significant role in determining the nature that boy-girl interactions are to take. The girl next door is either a cousin or a sister, thus getting a date becomes an acute problem. The questions that quickly surface are: "is it alright for cousins and kinsmen to date when the cultural norms demand otherwise? Where may the rural-based youth find dates?

The problem of finding a date, even for the rural-based youths, is not insurmountable, though, because dating is not just about mate selection, but it's also about friendship and the learning of social skills. There will be occasions when cousins or people who have blood ties will find themselves in circumstances that can pass for a dating situation.

When the motive is not sinister and mate-selection is not part of the deal, it is okay for people who are related by blood to date. It is alright for cousins to go out together on a Sabbath afternoon, for example, to appreciate nature. When it involves people who have blood ties, however, going out in a group is advisable. This will eliminate those compromising situations where the carnal nature wants to get the better of our sense of right and wrong.

But then dating is also about mate selection. There comes a time when a young person, more so the rural-based one, must be able to date a potential life partner. The question then recurs: where shall the rural-based youth find a date? Since it is true that we can only get to meet people as we travel, the rural-based youth might have to travel as resources allow, to meet a potential life partner. Travelling doesn't have to involve spending a lot of money. One does not need to travel too far to meet someone to date. It may sometimes involve no more than walking to the market centre in the neighbourhood or to the nearest town.

Joining a social group, a church group or a school club may also yield good results in the search for someone to date. By joining such groups, one gets to meet people, develop social skills and build self-esteem.

Sometimes the potential date is someone we meet everyday but we have never bothered to talk to. If one will find a date, he or she must talk. Talk to all potential dates you interact with everyday. Ask them out and try to know them well.

Visit your grandparents, an uncle, an aunt or any close relative during the school holidays. While there, try to make friends. This way, you will widen your network of friends.

Following the suggestions presented above should help take care of the problem of getting dates.

The problem of date rape
Rape is often understood in abstract terms as meaning that the one raped has never before met or seen the rapist. The picture created is of a weird looking man springing from

nowhere and pouncing on his victim, in most cases threatening to do harm to the victim should she raise an alarm. It is probably because of this understanding that it is difficult for people to accept that it is possible to become a victim of rape to someone well known and in circumstances that initially would appear unlikely to degenerate into this kind of abuse. The truth, however, is that it is possible for a victim to be raped by an acquaintance. Rape can occur during a date, when one partner coerces the other to engage in sexual intercourse against her will. This is referred to as date rape.

Date rape is a common phenomenon on the dating scene today. Many people would prefer to think of it in more polite terms as forced sex and not as rape. This is just a reflection of the thinking in our society today that presupposes it is not possible to rape someone you love. The thinking stipulates that no woman or girl, for that matter, would show signs of being ready for intercourse and that a little prodding must be done to set them in the mood. Intercourse, some people have reasoned, must seem to be forced for it to be more enjoyable.

Sometimes date rape is the result of coercion. Phrases such as, "if you love me, why don't you let me do it?" or "there is only one reason you don't want us to do it. It is because you don't love me" are common in boy-girl intimate relationships. And so the lady, wanting to prove her love for the young man, allows him to proceed with no more than mild protestations.

Society expects young men to be aggressive. This, the young people are expected to prove by the number of women they have "conquered," and conquering a woman is something to brag about. Then there is the attitude that when a lady says no, she actually means yes. This kind of attitude plays a role in the occurrence of date rape.

Date rape is sometimes the result of miscommunicated feelings or misunderstood signs. Some young men will take a longing look in the young woman's eyes or her allowing him to touch and kiss her as meaning "yes, I am ready for you." Taking cue from this, one thing leads to another and even the faint voice of protest from the woman will not deter him from cooling off the fires burning deep within him.

Drug abuse and the taking of alcohol is also a contributory factor to the reality of date rape. Drugs and alcohol have an intoxicating effect and tend to excite and stimulate nerves. They arouse feelings and excite an erotic response. Under the influence of drugs and alcohol, young people have found themselves doing things they would never do under sober conditions. Date rape is one such thing.

Date rape is an increasing reality in our society today. How may it be stopped? There are many ways of putting the prevalence of date rape under check. The beginning point has to do with a change in attitude. The attitudes that would seem to play a role in the causation of date rape must be changed. One example of such attitude is the one that makes men think that a lady's no means yes.

A clear distinction must be drawn between seduction and rape. Young men should appreciate and respond to the fact that it is gentlemanlike to seduce a lady, not to rape her. To force a lady into intercourse is not to love her; rather it is to abuse her.

It is important to be sure about feelings and to communicate the same effectively. The lady must learn to set limits and ensure that her partner respects the limits she has set. If she does not want any hands laid on her or to be caressed, she must learn to say, "hands off" with authority. If she does not want to be kissed, she must say so emphatically. Women must learn to say no in such a way that they would be understood to be saying so.

To avoid date rape resulting from lack of something constructive to do during the date, it is advisable to plan the activities for the date well in advance. Sometimes planning a group date can sufficiently take care of this.

Another way of helping stop date rape would be to be lucid early in the date whether you want it to turn sexual or not. If you don't intend it to be sexual, no gesture should be entertained that would seem to be pushing the date in the sexual direction.

It is, by and large, the responsibility of the girl to ensure that she is not raped since girls are in most cases the victims of date rape. The girl must resist all overtures of rape, using all means at her disposal. Such means include calmly talking him out of the idea, screaming, making herself unattractive in any reasonable way that would help turn the man off, or running away. If the man is unarmed, the girl may think of fighting him off physically, though this is risky since it could awaken the rogue in him. If the man is armed, it, however, may be prudent only to try to convict his humane side or awaken his sense of what is expected of a gentleman. It would be too risky to try to fight him off physically.

The emotional, psychological and physical consequences of rape, and more so date rape, are far-reaching. These include fear of being left alone, feelings of guilt, feelings of worthlessness, fear and distrust of all men, loss of interest in developing new relationships again, retreating into the world of fantasy away from the world of reality, and anxiety among others. It is, therefore, important that in the event of a rape in general and a date rape in particular, the healing process be put into effect immediately.

The very first thing to do is to stop seeing the rapist. One who cannot respect you enough to listen to your wishes and respect your position does not deserve your affection.

One needs the comfort and confidence of a loyal and trusted friend, more so in the days succeeding a rape. You need someone to talk to or someone you can bare all your anger and disgust, your worries and fears to. This aids the healing process. It enables you to release the pent-up emotions and start to live again. It is also advisable that the case is reported to law enforcement authorities, for rape, irrespective of the circumstances under which it occurred, is a criminal offence. Seeking legal redress helps to place the guilt where it belongs: on the rapist and not on the victim.

Owing to the trauma that usually accompanies events in our lives such as rape, seeking the help of a counsellor is useful in helping one to sort out feelings, putting the incident behind her and pressing forward into the future, since life must continue. The counsellor would be better placed to help the victim avoid self-recrimination and recognize that it could happen and indeed happened.

Seeking medical attention is also important, recognizing the reality of Sexually Transmitted Diseases and AIDS. The possibility of a bruise or any kind of damage to the victim's reproductive organs further necessitates the need to seek medical help immediately.

It is at this time that one craves family support more than at any other time. Being part of a family gives one the assurance of belonging. Talk to family members about the incident. Seek their understanding and support.

A vertical relationship with God will determine, to a great extent, how one goes through the therapeutic process. Such a relationship will help one learn to forgive, an act which, in itself, is therapeutic.

A relationship with God also enhances one's self-worth, and this is important in speeding up the healing process.

Unplanned dates

Unplanned dates are those that just happen without being pre-planned. It is those without a schedule of activities or events to take place during the date.

While there is no hard rule in dating, stipulating that there must be some kind of timetable for activities to be engaged in, or a program of events, for that matter, is a priority. It is helpful and wise to have an idea of how every minute will be spent while on a date.

Having a schedule of events helps take care of the boredom that might crop up during a date. Such boredom, especially where a couple is involved as opposed to group dating, could lead to other unintended activities. At the end of the outing, the couple may find it difficult to look at each other in the eye.

Planning dates also lifts pressure off the shoulders of those involved, concerning making impromptu decisions. More than that, it creates order and indicates that those involved are thoroughly organized. It is a reflection of who we are and an indication that we are not careless.

Unplanned dates are not a good idea. They are too risky, especially in a one-on-one situation. A lot of regrettable and yet avoidable things can happen during such dates.

Chapter Five

Dating and mate selection

Attraction toward another person, especially a person of the opposite sex, produces pleasant sensations. Such sensations may be so strong as to cause the one attracted to seek a relationship with the one he or she is attracted to. It is from this physical attractiveness that intimate relationships and life long unions find their root. It is also from physical attraction that a desire to "check out" and prove if the glitter is pure gold or base metal springs. Yet physical attraction alone must not be made the basis for entering into a dating relationship. There is need to consider inward beauty, which is more important than outward beauty.

Dating, as a process of socialization, may thus be considered as a series of casual and intimate involvements and interactions; as some form of sifting and filtration. It is this sifting process that yields partners for the life-long union. The dating process, therefore, involves a lot of study and requires a lot of prayer. It is also characterized by a lot of heartaches, and no one should be made to think that dating is a bed of roses or an easy ride. The path of dating is infested with thorns and thistles that prick those who tread it. It has sharp edges that bruise those who enter its confines. But it is a path that no one should be made to fear to walk, for it has its joys. One of the joys of dating is that it helps in the building of a sure foundation for marriage. The dating continuum represents a series of intimate interactions, characterized by joys and sorrows, but which eventually lead to total socialization and nuptial bliss.

During the dating process, every possible mate forms part of a testing experience. Since dating is understood to aid in the search for a marital partner, no assumption should be made that there can be only one true mate. This in no wise should make light the fact that a good wife or husband is the result of divine providence. God has made it possible for us to enjoy the companionship of each other through the spirit of true love that comes only from Him; for within and of themselves, human beings cannot be able to love as they really should.

The process of mate selection
The process of mate selection must involve keen and guided steps if mistakes are not to be made which would lead to regret and sorrow later, in married life.

Initially, people pair off due to observable features such as physical attractiveness. After the pairing off has taken place and the dating process is in motion, other things such as similarity in values, attitudes, opinions, interests and aspirations take over from physical attractiveness. Compatibility comes into consideration a little later in the relationship.

It has been observed that the dating process goes though a number of stages. After the pairing off, individuals begin to consider their degree of similarity in values, interests, opinions, appearances and needs as has already been mentioned. If enough similarities are discerned, rapport and interest take root. The partners begin to let each other into their 'cupboards' disclosing who they are to one another. Self-disclosure helps in assessing compatibility. The process of mate selection has been described as some kind of filtration process, whereby prospective dates are passed through a number of filters (Ketckhoff and Davis, 1962). According to Kerckhoff and Davis, the potential date is passed through six filters. These include:

- the nearness filter,
- the attractiveness filter,
- the social background filter,
- the complementarity filter,
- and the readiness for marriage filter.

The filtration process begins with a field of *eligibles*, that is; all the possible dating partners. These possible dating partners are passed through the nearness filter, because it is realistic that one can only date those who are accessible to him or her. Those possible dating partners who survive the nearness filter are then passed through the attractiveness filter because it is true that we can only date those we are attracted to physically. The filtration process moves on to the next filter, where similarities in social background are considered. Those who are not very similar to us in terms of social background are eliminated from the list, thus narrowing it down further. From the social background filter, the attitudes and values filter is brought into operation so that only those who share enough common interests, attitudes and value systems continue to date. The complementarity filter is then brought into play to weigh similarities in personality. The readiness for marriage filter comes last in the filtration process, only succeeded by marriage. The filtration process of mate selection may be represented on some kind of ladder as shown below.

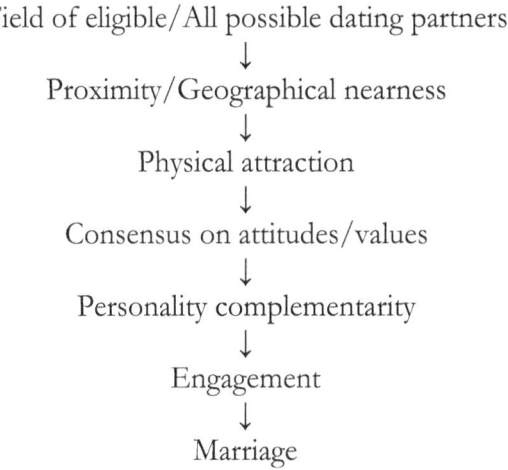

Field of eligible/All possible dating partners
↓
Proximity/Geographical nearness
↓
Physical attraction
↓
Consensus on attitudes/values
↓
Personality complementarity
↓
Engagement
↓
Marriage

The young man's shopping list

Ask any young man what tops the list of the things he would look for in a girl and physical beauty would be thrown at you without a second thought. It has been said that beauty is to man as intelligence is to a lady. But young men need to think beyond physical appearance when making the list of desirable qualities in that which will be flesh of your flesh and bone of your bones.

Experience shows that it would be wiser for the young man to regard the inward beauty of character more highly than the outward beauty.

Ellen G. White, author of The *Adventist Home*, notes that the young man considering linking his life-destiny with a young lady should be sure that the one with whom he wants to join in matrimony is fitted to bear her share of life's burdens. She should be one whose influence will ennoble and refine him.

The young man contemplating marriage should include the following questions in his shopping list:

- Will this lady make me happy in her love?
- Will she bring happiness or misery in the home that we will start?
- Will she be a good manager of our finances?
- Is she a lover of vain pleasure and appearance? If she is a lover of pleasure and appearance, it is unlikely she will manage family finances prudently.
- Will she be patient and forbearing with your mistakes?
- Will she treat you with understanding?
- Will she be willing to care for your mother in her old age?
- Will she be possessive such that she withdraws you from society or will she help widen your network of friends?
- Does she have a teachable spirit?

- Will a union with her help you grow heavenward? Will the union increase your love for God or will it cause you to backslide?
- Does she live a prayerful life? Does she make important decisions based on moral and divine principles?

If a Christian young man is to reap joy and not sorrow from marriage, he would do well to give the above questions serious consideration.

The young lady's shopping list
Many girls go for temporal things in men. They fall for physical appearance rather than for the beauty of character that lasts. Height, weight, complexion, intonation and type of hair appeal to many young ladies more than the qualities of character such as patience, humility, kindness, love, tenderness, diligence, intelligence and spiritual commitment. Such choices have caused many a young woman sorrow and misery when she could enjoy the blessing of a peaceful and happy union just by inviting God to make the choices for her and help her set her priorities right.

Ellen G. White, in the book *Fundamentals of Christian Education,* suggests a number of questions a young lady should ask herself before accepting to join in marriage with a young man. Does the young man have a mother? What is the stamp of her character on him? Does he recognize his obligation to his mother? Is he mindful of her wishes and desires; her happiness and joy? Does he respect his mother?

It should be noted that if the young man does not respect and honour his mother, chances are high that he will not respect his wife either. He will not manifest love, kindness and affection toward his wife if he cannot do the same to his mother.

Following are further questions that a young lady should ask before accepting to unite in marriage with a young man:

- When the novelty of marriage is over, will he still show love and affection to me?
- Will he be forbearing with my mistakes or will he be the critical type, overbearing and dictatorial?
- Is he spiritually committed?
- Does he have room for prayer?
- Are you compatible in values, goals and personality?
- Do your parents and friends approve of your relationship?
- Does the young man have a teachable spirit?
- Is he willing and humble enough to recognize his weaknesses and strive to change?
- Do you feel that God approves of your relationship with this man?
- Are you at peace with God, yourself and with your friends and relatives about your relationship?
- Do you feel safe and secure with this man?
- Can you trust him?
- Do you love him?

These questions should be able to help a young lady make a 'winning' shopping list. It is unlikely that a young man about whom the answers to these questions are in the affirmative would make a poor husband.

Breaking up

While it is not easy for two people who have known each other and interacted quite closely for a period of time to say 'goodbye,' the fact is that breaking up is sometimes inevitable. It is important for young people who are dating to know that there will always come a time when the best thing to do is to break up.

As crushing as it is, breaking up should not only be seen as a painful experience that puts an end to a relationship. Rather, it is in more than one way God's beautiful way of telling us that there is someone better along the road for us.

Dating, as a mate selection process, has been likened to a test drive. In as much as the buyer is under no compulsion to buy a car proved to be defective after the test drive, even so, it's okay not to marry anyone your dating experience has given you the impression you two would not be happy together. It is okay to get out of a relationship in which you have reason to believe you are not being adequately prepared to be of service to humanity and to God, for that is the essence of our human relatedness. The question that needs to be answered, therefore, is not whether it is okay to break up or not; rather the question to be addressed is: what is the best way to break up?

The best way for Christian young people to break up is to begin with God. Because God has been at the centre of the relationship, His will and insight should be sought even when a break up seems inevitable. If it is God's will that the break up should wait, then those involved must be willing to wait. Similarly, if it is that the break up be effected right away, then it must be effected in that manner. But even when the break up must be effected, it should be handled with tact. Breaking up, it should be remembered, is not about embarrassing or disgracing the one you are breaking up with. Whatever the reason or reasons for the break up, it is important, first and foremost, to be honest and let the one you are breaking up with know exactly why a break up is inevitable. It is a Christian duty to help the other person understand and accept what is happening.

Before moving ahead with the break up, it is wise to seek counsel from older friends who can be trusted. Whatever advises they offer should not be regarded lightly or ignored, but should be considered seriously.

Breaking up with someone you have been dating does not mean that you have become enemies. In as much as breaking up hurts and causes heartache, it is important to part as friends. This does not mean that the decision to break up should be put on the hold for the sake of friendship. Once the decision has been made to break up, the break up should be effected with a sense of finality. It hurts more to give the one with whom you are breaking up signals that it is not truly over. Don't call, send gifts or write letters. These will make it difficult for you to get over each other and start on the healing process. In fact, it may even be necessary to stay clear off each other for a period of time as a further aid to the healing process.

The decision to break up should be communicated quietly and with feeling. It should be done in such a way that the wounded partner is not brought to public scorn and shame. Whatever wrongs have been committed should be forgiven. Thank each other for the moments you have shared and for the blessings you have reaped from the relationship. It is not advisable to go down on your knees and beg the one breaking up with you to take you back. Similarly, promising to become what the person breaking up with you wants you to be is not wise either. Neither is it wise to resort to crying or even to threaten that you would commit suicide if the person does not take you back. Groaning and brooding over your hurt won't help anything. As a matter of fact, it will only make you bitter and such bitterness might just cause you to lose your perspective on life and eventually lead to your ruin.

The Bible says, in Isaiah 40:31, that "…they that wait upon the Lord shall renew their strength; they shall mount up with wings as eagles; they shall run and not be weary; and they shall walk and not faint." It pays to wait upon God and to trust Him even when our circumstances seem so hopeless. We can trust Him to take care of our pain and give us a new lease of life to continue going. Most important, it's rewarding to note that a break up may be God's way of telling us that He has someone special for us.

Chapter Six

Are you ready to tie the knot?

When is one ready for marriage? How can you be sure that you are ready for marriage? Answers to these questions are not easy to come by. It is important to note that being ready for marriage is not always determined by chronological age alone, though this is important.

Being ready for marriage is not just a feeling. It is a decision backed up by principles. It is a decision made with regard to one's circumstances and the dictates of the social, cultural and economic environment. It is, therefore, right to say that if a young man, after a thorough consideration of his social, cultural, economic or even religious circumstances, decides to marry at fifteen, it is alright. Similarly, it is alright for a man to turn forty before getting married if that is a comfortable and right decision, depending on his assessed circumstances. One is not ready for marriage simply because his or her age mates are all married.

Marriage is an important phenomenon in our lives. It is regarded severally as a rite of passage, as an end, or as an experience that every normal male and female must go through at a given point in life. Marriage is the culmination of premarital intimate male-female interactions. It is the consummation of intense human love, leading to a oneness that cannot be achieved otherwise. It is sacred and divinely ordained.

The foregoing declaration, though brief for now, emphasizes why it is absolutely necessary that marriage should be entered into on a sound premise. The dating process should help in the building of such a premise. It is, therefore, appropriate that this chapter focus attention on this important event in our lives. This chapter seeks to answer the questions: How can you tell if it is true love? An honest and affirmative answer to this question is useful in helping determine compatibility, which is profoundly important in marriage. Statistics indicate that divorce is on the rise at an alarming rate, and many are left wondering whether the marriage institution will survive. Some people have argued that it will probably be more appropriate to reword the vow "till death do us part" to read "till divorce do us part." But let me leave that alone for now. The other question we need to answer is: is marriage still worth it or has it lost its nobility?

How to differentiate true love from infatuation

Telling whether it is true love or infatuation is not easy. This is so because it is true of both to involve feelings and it is never easy to tell whether feelings are true or untrue. And yet it is important that those contemplating marriage be sure that it is true love and not infatuation binding them if they are not to reap sorrow, pain and misery from the marriage.

True love is a choice; it is not just a happening. While it is true that there may, and indeed should be feelings, true love is not just based on feelings and affections alone. It is the result of nurture and nourishment. It is the outcome of a long period of interaction and study. It does not happen overnight. It is not just a first sight attraction, an impulse, an intense feeling of a fondness. It is a high principle, indeed a decision.

True love involves devotion and commitment. Such devotion and commitment should not be one-sided. Both partners must be devoted and committed to each other and to the relationship. It should be a matter of needing somebody who needs you; of loving somebody who loves you. Love, it has been said, thrives where there is love. True love is, therefore, the product of a garden planted, watered and nurtured by both partners. It is like a plant that must be tended to bear good fruit. Love, and not just love as such, but true love and strong love, is the only sound premise upon which marriage may be entered into. And to love strong enough involves forsaking all others and choosing to love only one with both mind and heart. It involves making a choice out of many attractions. True love should be able to recognize that it is possible to admire many members of the opposite sex, but it must be able to make a choice and abide by the choice made.

True love is calm, patient, gentle, humble, tolerant and never rash. It is not born out of strong passion, and neither is it driven by erotic sentimentalism alone. It does not regard the outward appearance as everything, but regards the inward adornments of character highly.

True love is moral. It is able to separate chaff from noble ideals. It never trivializes serious matters such as matters of love. It is not blind. What is blind is infatuation. It is infatuation that cannot see beyond the surface. Infatuation just knows that he is handsome or that she is beautiful; that there are strong feelings; that there is something in me that wants her, but I cannot tell what it is.

Infatuation reasons, 'Lets get married while the fire lasts, if we prolong the relationship, we might fall out of love' or 'I have this feeling deep inside me. It must be love.' Tue love is able to tell what it is that binds two people of the opposite sex together.

Intense feelings are sometimes experienced with true love. But the feelings do not rule over the intellect. The heart does not get the better of the head. Rather, the head rationalizes the desires of the heart. True love is predisposed to a sense of release and openness toward each other. It communicates feelings, shares its joys and sorrows, does not hide its fears and cherishes respect. It is ennobling, enabling and empowering.

It is not true love if it demands a reward. True love keeps flowing in spite of mistakes, shortcomings and weaknesses. It seeks to correct the mistakes, eradicate the shortcomings and replace the weaknesses with real strength, whether moral, physical or intellectual. True love is a gift of God. It is not within us to show the kind of disinterested love that true love is supposed to be. Indeed, it is not human nature to love, but God's. True love is, therefore, a gift which once received must be nurtured and cultivated.

Gauging compatibility

It is important for two people intending to get into a life-long relationship to be sure that they are compatible. Compatibility, however, should not be understood to mean that the two are similar in all ways. It does mean that they need to have enough similarities; that their interests and value systems are not far apart.

As has been noted in chapter five, compatibility involves sharing similarities in a number of crucial areas. Such include race, tribe, religious convictions, social background, economic background, career and social goals, sex-role expectations and moral values, among others. These must be considered in gauging the level of compatibility. It should be noted, however, that marriages have succeeded where the couple do not share same background in terms of race or tribe. Nevertheless, such marriages are the exception and not the rule. While it is true that before God there is neither Jew nor Gentile, meaning that we are one, yet race and tribe still count heavily in determining the success chances of any marriage. In gauging compatibility, it is important to note that no one is a perfect mate. No two people can be perfectly suited for each other that areas of conflict never arise. Compatibility is, therefore, guided by the twin words, acceptability and adaptability. In determining the level of compatibility, it is wise to consider the following questions:

- Are you ready and wiling to accept and live with the mistakes, faults and shortcomings of the one with whom you are intending to link your life?

Are you ready to tie the knot?—101

- Do you share enough interests in common?
- Are your career and social goals compatible?
- Do your social and moral values tie close enough?
- Can you say with conviction that your partner is suited to meet the roles demanded by marriage?
- Do you have a realistic estimation of yourselves?
- Are both of you ready and willing to commit yourselves to a life-long union?
- Have you discovered who you are and does your partner agree with your estimation of yourself?
- Are you friends enough? It is a time-tested truism that you marry your best friend
- Do you feel that you are fully accepted by your partner?
- Are both of you wiling to make sacrifices to make the relationship work?
- Are you physically attracted to each other? It is true that there can only be a complete and fulfilling union of bodies with the heart's acceptance.
- Have you fully gotten over your past 'hurt' and are you willing to give yourselves fully and completely to each other?
- If you were given a second chance to make another choice, would you still choose this partner and not another one?

Answering these questions in the affirmative would predict very high chances of compatibility.

Chapter Seven

Wrapping up

Some people join the dating game because their friends or peers are dating. This is a wrong reason to date. Dating should be your initiative. Don't date because others expect you to. If you have not found the person you want to go out with, wait. It is not wise to go out with just anyone, but keep old friends even as you make new ones.

Dating, first and foremost, is not so much about marriage as it is about friendship. There is a danger in getting too involved and thinking that once you start going out, the next stop is the altar. Not all dating relationships culminate into marriage. Take advantage of the ease and freedom that the dating game provides to learn about yourself and about those you date as you prepare for marriage. If, through your dating relationships, you end up finding one suited for you, go ahead and tie the knot.

Dating is not about allowing the emotional fires within us to explode. It is not a way of escaping the reality of our sexual passions through cheap sex. Dating is about being moral and respecting each other as male and female. For some people, dating is a compulsion; a tyrant ruling their lives with an iron fist. This should not be the case. Rather, dating should complement our daily lives. It should form part of the activities we engage in during leisure. Better still, it should be one of the activities we make time for.

Dating is not a limiting activity. It should not shrink our horizons. When we date, it does not follow that we should say goodbye to old friends because we have met someone special we want to devote all our time to. On the contrary, dating should widen our scope of interactions. Dating is about making friends. It is meant to enrich our lives rather than limit us.

How do you know you've met the special person?
Getting to know that you have found someone to date and possibly marry is not easy. Many young people would rather wait until they are absolutely sure rather than go out with 'just anybody.' When it is noted that dating is, first and foremost, about knowing people better rather than getting involved in a commitment, the range of choices is widened. In essence, therefore, young people do not have to wait until that 'special someone' chances to come by before they can begin to date.

There comes a time, however, when you want to move in a specific direction and you want to be sure that it is the 'special person.' Perhaps you have been involved with a number of dates and you feel that it is time to begin moving in the direction of a serious relationship, and probably marriage. Here are a few tips that can help you know that you have found 'the one of your dreams.'

- It is the person who catches your attention in a special way; the one you find yourself wanting to spend a lot of time with.

- It is the one you have the longing to get to know better.
- That special person for you might be the one who challenges and intrigues you; the one you get the feeling has a mystery about him or her which you cannot understand but which you would wish to unravel.
- That special someone is not the person whose interests and value system is similar to yours in every way, nonetheless, he/she is the one you share enough common interests with.
- He/she is the one in whose company you feel at peace with yourself, with others and with God.
- He/she is the one you can disagree with and still afford to come together and forgive each other.
- That special someone could be that person who challenges you and makes you yearn to grow emotionally, socially and spiritually.
- He/she is the one who gets the approval of your friends and family.
- He/she is the one you respect and would not want to hurt.
- He/she is the one who is responsible enough not to be bent on having your relationship take the form of the debased and physical.
- He/she is the one who has a teachable spirit. He or she is ready to learn and does not have a know-it-all attitude.

Point to ponder
What are you looking for in a premarital male-female relationship? Won't you be better-off not being in such a relationship? Male-female premarital relationships, especially of the romantic nature, can be quite a headache!

Make Notes Here:

www.ingramcontent.com/pod-product-compliance
Lightning Source LLC
Chambersburg PA
CBHW031652040426
42453CB00006B/275